Table of Contents

Chapter 1: Pisces Personality Profile

Ruling planet: Neptune

Symbol: the two fishes

Element: water

Quality: mutable

Pisces Traits: brilliant, changeable, chaotic, compassionate, creative, escapist, idealistic, imaginative, intriguing, introspective, introverted, intuitive, moody, self-sacrificing, sensitive, talented, trusting

Brilliant

Pisceans are often brilliant in some way, with many displaying scientific or artistic genius. Pisceans are overrepresented among the scientists and inventors (Nicolaus Copernicus, Albert Einstein, Alexander Graham Bell, and Steve Jobs were all Pisceans) and among those with artistic talents, such Pierre-Auguste Renoir and Michelangelo Buonarroti. Plenty of Pisceans are also good dancers or singers, and most have beautiful or unusual voices (Pisces singers include Rihanna, Kurt Cobain, Nat King Cole, Kesha, Queen Latifah, Lou Reed, Justin Bieber, Nina Simone, and Johnny Cash).

The challenge for Pisceans lies in harnessing their considerable creative or innovative energies. The intensity of feeling that comes with this sign can drive them to achieve great things, but it can also act as a barrier to achievement if they become so overwhelmed with depression or anxiety that it is hard to do anything at all.

Pisceans who experience overly intense emotional states should seek creative outlets that are distracting and therapeutic. The bouts of intense sadness or anxiety many Pisceans suffer can often be channeled into brilliant creative or innovative works.

Changeable

Pisceans sometimes appear fickle or unreliable because they change their minds so frequently. What they wanted very much one day may repel them the next, and some even seem to be drastically different people from day to day.

Because their feelings and preferences are so changeable, Pisceans tend to make huge, life-altering changes in response to particularly intense feelings or shifts in preference, unless their ascendants are in more stable signs (for example, Taurus or Capricorn). With such mutable emotions, desires, and sense of self, they do best with friends and partners who act as anchors, providing stability and reassurance as needed and preventing them from doing anything too impulsive and self-destructive.

Pisceans also tend to change their appearances many times over the course of their lives, and some can even look quite different at various times of the day or week. Most love costumes and disguises. They enjoy the intrigue of secret identities and feel safer when hidden behind a mask, whether that mask is physical or psychological. This tendency to hide can make Pisceans difficult to know or understand, as they show their true selves to very few people.

Compassionate

Unless their ascendants are in less sensitive signs, Pisceans tend to be kind-hearted champions of the underdog, willing to do anything to help those who are physically or emotionally suffering. They also have natural healing abilities, which draw some into medicine, nursing, or naturopathic fields.

Pisceans can endure almost anything if it will help someone else, and they will assist any sick, vulnerable, or stray being who needs them. They tend to be happiest when involved in charity or volunteer work of some sort, and in their personal lives, they are inclined to take care of friends, relatives, and even strangers or animals that come their way. Because they are somewhat gullible, they may be deceived or used by people who take advantage of their sympathetic natures.

Pisceans can be very courageous when protecting and defending others. While they often choose not to stand up to bullies on their own behalf, they can display impressive bravery when another vulnerable person or an animal is at risk.

Conflict-avoidant

Pisceans can usually see the validity of two truths simultaneously, so they have difficulty taking sides (unless one individual in the conflict is vulnerable or disadvantaged, in which case the Piscean will usually defend the underdog). The tendency to see the validity of two different truths, combined with their sensitive natures and fear of hurting others, causes Pisceans to avoid conflict whenever possible, preferring to act as peacemakers is contentious situations.

Typical Pisceans will avoid doing or saying anything hurtful, even if it is warranted. They suffer intense guilt over small things and psychologically torture themselves in response to minor incidents. Because they are sensitive and dislike hurting others, they are inclined to compromise, soothe fiery tempers, or simply escape to defuse potentially explosive situations.

Pisceans can be incredibly heroic when defending a vulnerable individual or group against cruelty or oppression. However, in their personal lives, they find fighting extremely distressing and will retreat, emotionally and physically, from companions who try to discuss difficult issues or pick fights.

A softly, softly approach is required when discussing emotionally charged issues with a Pisces partner, friend, or family member. Blunt or harsh interactions will drive an emotional wedge between the Piscean and his or her companion, and this breach may never be healed.

Creative

Pisceans are among the most creative signs of the zodiac. The beloved writers Douglas Adams and Dr. Seuss and the brilliant composers Frederic Chopin and Antonio Vivaldi were born under the sign of Pisces.

Many Pisceans gravitate to creative pursuits to relieve stress because they have discovered that the best way to weather emotional storms without getting pulled under is to immerse themselves in engaging activities.

Pisceans are often drawn to arts and crafts or the maker movement, which focuses more on invention, tinkering, and technical innovation. Some also express their creative talents through singing and/or song writing, dancing, or other activities that can be classified as body arts, or through building, renovation, and decoration.

Escapist

Pisceans are the daydreamers of the zodiac, escaping difficult or boring situations through any means possible. As a result, they are vulnerable to developing addictions to various things, including alcohol, food, television, movies, videogames, work, or creative pursuits (these activities can be classified as addictions when the Piscean does them so continuously and obsessively that other areas of life are neglected or health suffers).

Although Pisceans will care for others in extreme adversity, they have difficulty caring for themselves, both psychologically and physically. They can easily lose track of the collective reality if they drink too much or abuse other substances, which exacerbates their existing tendency to drift off into pleasurable daydreams.

Fortunately, many Pisceans have a physical intolerance for drugs or alcohol, which may save them from developing substance abuse problems. However, addiction to food is a common problem for this sign, and many Pisceans must fight their tendency to overindulge in tasty treats (and the associated weight gain).

Idealistic

Pisceans have many fine qualities, but social realism is not among them. Instead, they tend to see everything as either wonderful or terrible, leading to constant disappointment for overly optimistic Pisceans and depression for those who take a more pessimistic view of the world.

Unless they have succumbed to depression, Pisceans tend to be idealistic about the nature and behavior of those around them. They believe that people can and will change for the better, and that those who are behaving badly will improve with support and love.

A propensity for idealism enables Pisceans to labor tirelessly on behalf of the unfortunate. Although they can achieve wonderful things if they put their energies behind a good cause, their desire to help others leaves them vulnerable to being exploited by any sociopath with a good sob story.

Imaginative

Pisceans have vivid imaginations, which are both a source of creativity and a means of escape from unpleasant situations. Properly harnessed, their imaginative faculties can inspire the creation of wonderful things. However, having a very active imagination can also lead to a creative rewriting of history in the minds of Pisceans, or cause them to have unrealistic expectations of others.

Pisceans may be accused of lying when their accounts don't match with other people's memories of events. However, these discrepancies are more likely to occur because Piscean imaginations are so powerful that they confuse fantasy with reality or because they deceive themselves to avoid painful truths, not because they actually want to deceive or manipulate others.

Pisceans are great visualizers, so they can benefit from envisioning what they want to achieve to boost their confidence and increase the likelihood of success. They can also use their impressive imaginations to make mundane activities more fun so that they can escape the dullness of dreary routines. However, their imaginations are so powerful that there is a risk of getting lost in a fantasyland. Staying sufficiently grounded in the real world can be a challenge.

Intriguing

Pisceans have an indefinable, captivating quality that fascinates others, drawing people into their orbit. While some are baffled by the unusual Piscean personality, many are intrigued.

Pisceans have certain intangible attributes that capture the imagination of those who encounter them. Whether they are liked or disliked, others rarely find them boring or ordinary, and they have the potential to become sources of inspiration for those around them.

One particular aspect of the Piscean nature that contributes to this sign's natural intrigue is the tendency to be secretive. Pisceans hide aspects of their personalities from others (and even from themselves, in many cases). They have hidden depths, and what others see is only the tip of the iceberg. Their secretiveness can make them appear mysterious, and their elusive natures frustrate some while enchanting others who want to discover what lies beneath the enigmatic exterior.

Introspective

Pisceans are highly introspective, to the point where they can disappear into their own minds. They obsess over their private thoughts and feelings, sometimes to an unhealthy degree, increasing the risk of developing depression or anxiety.

Pisces is a sign that needs distraction to avoid negative rumination, and exercise and creative and innovative pursuits can prevent Pisceans from torturing themselves with repetitive unhappy or fearful thoughts. Positive distractions are very important for Pisceans, as they are needed to maintain mental and physical health.

Pisceans have a strong need for solitary time to process their thoughts and feelings and recharge their batteries after periods of socializing, and while some time alone is beneficial, too much can be problematic because it contributes to the tendency toward depressive or anxious rumination. Pisceans need good people in their lives to distract them when they are unhappy, and to provide a reality check if they start to slip into fantasy worlds.

Introverted

Pisceans are receptive to a wide variety of energies, both good and bad. They can catch the moods of others like viruses and pick up emotions by proximity, which is why they need more time alone than those of other signs.

Pisceans go through alternating sociable and reclusive phases, retreating from the world when their craving for solitude kicks in. Without sufficient alone-time, they can become emotionally drained, psychologically distressed, or even physically ill.

A major challenge for Pisceans is to determine the ideal amount of time to spend in their social and solitary states, as they need everything finely balanced to maintain optimal mental and physical health.

Intuitive

Pisceans often pick up on the feelings of others even when there are no outward signs that another person is upset (or the outward signs point in the opposite direction because the individual is putting on a brave face). They can identify those in need of support and kindness and respond as required. However, many Pisceans can sense malevolence in others as well, picking up on some underlying badness that others aren't registering.

Some Pisceans experience weird waking states or bizarre dreams that are sometimes prophetic. Many also have unusual experiences, such as seeing ghosts or encountering other inexplicable phenomena. Piscean intuition is quite powerful, and it often alerts them to danger or growing problems before there is solid evidence that something is wrong.

Pisceans prefer to make decisions based on gut feelings rather than weighing up the objective pros and cons of a situation. They get an instant sense of rightness or wrongness about particular people, situations, or choices, and they are inclined to trust their own intuition rather than what is said to them by others.

Moody

Pisceans experience very dark psychological states as well as periods of intense joy. They sink incredibly low and come bouncing back up with shocking speed, and their moods may fluctuate wildly from one extreme to another many times in a single day.

The mood swings they experience can be a great creative force, but there is a risk that Pisceans will be pulled under by a tide of despair. Sympathetic, supportive partners, friends, and family members can help to mitigate the risk that a sad mood will trigger a downward trajectory that continues on to depression.

Prone to Extremes

The symbol for Pisces depicts two fish swimming in opposite directions, and this is an accurate metaphor for the Pisces nature.

Pisceans often find themselves pulled in two different directions, always trying to balance but prone to swinging from one extreme to the other. For example, some Pisceans are impractical and irresponsible, squandering their money on silly things, while others are financially cautious to the point of miserliness. Pisceans also tend to be either extremely careful or prone to taking excessive risks with their health and safety, and to be very kind or merciless (although the former is more typical—while most Pisceans are compassionate by nature, a small proportion are capable of remarkable greed and cruelty, and their ability to read the emotions of others helps them use and abuse their victims).

Because Pisceans are prone to extremes and tend to make decisions based on intuition rather than observable evidence, many favor blind faith over reason. They like to feel their way through a situation, and they develop very strong, unshakable belief systems. When Pisceans have faith in a person, a system, or an ideology, it is very difficult to persuade them to change their minds. On the other hand, if they have not yet formed an impression, they are very open-minded, able to consider a variety of perspectives.

Whether Pisceans gravitate to one extreme or another will depend on other elements in their natal zodiacs.*

---

* The natal zodiac refers to the positions of the planets in the sky at the time of birth. Important influences in the natal zodiac include the sun sign (the one most people know), the moon sign, and the rising sign (also known as the ascendant). Other elements in the natal zodiac can influence how the sun sign is expressed. For example, a Pisces with Sagittarius rising would be less sensitive than a typical Pisces.

Some Pisceans oscillate between two opposing extremes, never finding a reasonable middle ground.

Self-sacrificing

Pisceans are inclined to sacrifice their own desires to those of others, and this can lead to the development of a resentful martyr complex if they're not careful. They must take time out for themselves and attend to their own needs at least some of the time to prevent this from happening.

Pisceans frequently get dumped on by others and usually don't refuse unreasonable requests, so they can be taken advantage of until they reach the point where they snap, becoming emotionally distressed or displaying a rare burst of rage. Cultivating some healthy assertiveness is beneficial for this sign, and some Pisceans learn this early on, developing a tough exterior to hide their vulnerability.

The positive side of the Piscean tendency toward self-sacrifice is a heroic nature. Pisceans are inclined to sacrifice their own health and safety to save those who are in need or in danger, a trait that draws some

Pisceans into professions that involve taking personal risks to rescue or care for others.

Sensitive

Pisceans are sensitive to rejection, criticism, and other forms of negative feedback. They are also sensitive to the feelings of others, so most will avoid cruelty (though the rare cruel Pisceans can be particularly deadly because their sensitivity enables them to discern the secret feelings and fears of other people and exploit them).

Pisceans are also very sensitive to environments, so they need to be cautious about where they choose to live and work, as well as who they spend their time with. They do best with stable, sensible friends and romantic partners who act as solid anchors in their lives, preventing them from drifting off into fantasy, depression, or anxious obsession.

Talented

Pisceans are overrepresented among the gifted and talented. This arises partly from innate nature but is also attributable to Piscean obsessiveness and escapist tendencies.

When Pisceans find something they're good at or that makes them feel good, they'll usually spend an enormous amount of time pursuing the activity because it provides therapy for negative mood states. Pisceans also need plenty of time either alone or working quietly side-by-side with trusted companions, which ensures that they get plenty of practice with their chosen activity. The result is that any underlying talent becomes well-developed over time.

Trusting

Pisceans are vulnerable to being exploited, both monetarily and emotionally, because they are trusting, naïve, and idealistic, unless their ascendants fall in more cynical signs. A tough rising sign can protect a Piscean against this sort of abuse, but without this shield, Pisceans can be taken advantage of by unscrupulous individuals.

Although they are repelled by the sort of charming sociopaths who brag and behave in an overconfident manner, manipulators who present themselves as victims can capture Piscean sympathies. Most Pisceans will respond with kindness and generosity to those they believe have been mistreated or have suffered a bout of terrible luck, so con artists can exploit Piscean compassion if they push the right buttons. A major challenge for this sign is developing a healthy scepticism when presented with compelling sob stories by those who seek financial support or other forms of help.

The Atypical Pisces

The sun sign isn't the only element in the natal zodiac that influences personality. Aspects and planetary placements, particularly the moon sign and rising sign (ascendant), are also important. For example, a Pisces with Taurus rising will be more stable and practical than a typical Pisces, and with Aquarius rising, a Piscean will be less sensitive and secretive, and the desire to care for others will be more likely to manifest as participation in projects, political movements, or other activities focused on helping large groups of people rather than focusing on single individuals in need.

There are many websites that offer free chart calculation to determine other planetary placements and aspects. Learning about these other factors is recommended, as it provides a more comprehensive personality profile.

See Appendix 2 for information about other astrological influences on personality and how to find your ascendant, moon sign, and other planetary placements.

Chapter 2: Pisces Love and Friendship Style

Pisceans have intangible qualities that draw others to them, as well as the intuitive ability to pick up on the mental states of those around them, which makes them appealing and sympathetic companions. Because they have a need to be needed, they often befriend or fall in love with those who require help and support (however, some Pisceans take on the dependent role, seeking rescuers for friendship and romantic partnerships). The powerful urge to care for and rescue others can have beautiful or ugly results, depending on whether the other person is deserving of this care and focus.

When a Piscean is able to rescue a deserving individual, the friendship or romantic relationship can be rewarding for both. However, when others fake conditions or situations to gain attention or resources, Pisceans can waste a lot of time and energy on them.

Many Pisceans seek excitement or intensity, even though this isn't good for them. They do far better with trustworthy, practical, earthy types than the insensitive and irresponsible individuals they are often drawn to. However, although the disappointments that result from poor choices may bring them down for a time, Pisceans have remarkable powers of self-regeneration, and when they focus their attentions on those who are worthy of their love and friendship, deep and beautiful connections can be forged.

Relationship Strengths

Unless their own lives are in a disastrous state, Pisceans are excellent companions for those in crisis, as they are sympathetic to the feelings of others and will minister to those in need with great kindness and patience. They are also diplomatic and tolerant of other people's quirks and flaws, often showing the greatest sympathy and understanding when others are at their worst.

Typical Pisceans are open-minded and nonjudgmental, which makes them great confidants. They look for the good in others and give people many chances (far too many in some cases), a trait that unscrupulous types may take advantage of.

Most Pisceans will not abandon a friend or partner in need. Instead, they are selfless with their time and energy and emotionally generous as well, putting their own needs and feelings aside to care for others.

Pisceans make particularly good companions for other introverts because they are happy to spend a lot of time on their own interests and hobbies. They do not require entertaining and make few social demands. All they ask is that others be kind and allow them the space they need to do their own thing when they need to recharge their social batteries.

Relationship Challenges

Pisceans may be hard to know or confusing to those around them because they can be deceptive about their feelings, in many cases even hiding painful or distressing things from themselves as well as others. This is usually done to prevent conflict or avoid hurting friends, family members, or partners, though it may serve the Piscean's own interests as well.

Because they are so sensitive, Pisceans are easily hurt and they must work hard to protect themselves. Many Pisceans (particularly men) adopt a tough exterior to hide their vulnerability. Typical Pisceans find it easier to endure physical pain than the emotional suffering that comes from unhealthy, broken, or lost relationships.

Another relationship challenge for Pisceans arises from their desire to feel that they are making a difference in someone else's life. Although they like to have an anchor (a person who is solid, sane, and reasonable, whom they can count on), many are drawn to high-intensity people who bring turmoil to their lives. Some choose partners who are helpless, incompetent, disadvantaged, addicted, temperamental, or mentally ill because they have a strong desire to help those who are suffering. As a result, they can end up squandering their emotional and physical energies on people who are the authors of their own misfortunes and unlikely to change, even when provided with the support necessary to do so.

Pisceans often choose dramatic or chaotic partners and friends, despite the fact that they are somewhat chaotic themselves (which is usually reflected in their cluttered homes). They are inclined to favor passionate relationships over stable ones, which can lead to heartbreak.

Many Pisceans seem to thrive on strife, wandering off when things calm down and the friend or lover seems to be doing well. This stems from the Piscean desire to be needed; if Pisceans feel that their companions are fine without them, they tend to redirect their energies toward those who can benefit from their care. As a result, they may abandon the stable relationships that are good for them, instead seeking the company of those who have a negative impact on their mental and physical health.

Chapter 3: Pisces Compatibility With Other Sun Signs

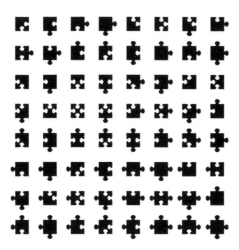

Note: There is more to astrological compatibility than sun signs alone. Other elements in a person's natal zodiac also play a role. Ascendants (rising signs), moon signs, and other planetary placements and aspects also shape personality and affect compatibility. For example, a Capricorn with Leo rising will be more extroverted than a typical Capricorn, and a Sagittarius with Taurus rising or the moon in Scorpio will be more compatible with Pisces than a typical Sagittarius. For more information on other natal chart elements, see Appendix 2.

Pisces + Aries

This match can be difficult. In a worst-case scenario, Aries may find Pisces too indecisive, sensitive, and secretive, while Pisces finds Aries cruel, selfish, and domineering. On the other hand, if other elements in their natal zodiacs are compatible, these two can form a nice complement to one another and develop a deep, intense connection. However, for this match to work, Pisces will probably need to toughen up a bit and Aries will have to develop some verbal restraint and sensitivity.

On the plus side, Aries may be fascinated by the intriguing Pisces personality, while Pisces appreciates the bold forcefulness of Aries. In a positive relationship, Pisces will lean on Aries for support when besieged by bleak moods and dire circumstances, and Aries will find respite from the relentless stress of fighting to be on top in the company of tolerant Pisces (typical Pisceans have no urge to dominate or control others). Aries can help Pisces become bolder (or at least act as a screen behind which Pisces can hide), and Pisces can help Aries develop latent intuitive and creative faculties.

Lifestyle conflicts may arise with this pairing because Pisces tends to be more introverted and likes to spend more time either at home, in the homes of trusted friends, or out in nature, whereas the typical Aries cultivates a broader social circle. Pisces is easily overwhelmed by noise and chaos, whereas Aries thrives in overly stimulating environments. These two may disagree about preferred activities, with the result that Aries goes off in search of more boisterous companions and Pisces stays at home, feeling insecure. When this pair fight, Pisces is likely to get the worst of it because Aries tends to speak impulsively, blurting things out in the heat of the moment that leave lasting scars (Aries can also be hurt by conflict, but tends to get over it quickly).

Despite the problems associated with this match, Aries and Pisces do have some traits that can bring them together. Both signs tend to be altruistic and generous in their positive manifestations (even to the point of courageous self-sacrifice), and Aries strength can form a nice complement to Pisces intuition. Both also tend to be creative, which be a basis for shared interests. However, whether or not these two create a beautiful balance together or their relationship is blown apart by conflict will likely depend on the compatibility of other elements in their natal zodiacs. If their ascendants and moon signs don't mesh, the Aries tendency to verbally attack when frustrated combined with the Piscean tendency to escape in search of greener pastures when things grow difficult may pull these two apart.

Pisces + Taurus

This can be a beautiful combination. These two tend to be very compatible and their relationship should be harmonious unless there is something seriously wrong with one of the participants (such as a drug or alcohol addiction) or other elements of their natal zodiacs are highly incompatible.

Taurus and Pisces form a nice complement to one another. The Taurus strength, stability, calmness, and decisiveness act as an anchor for Pisces, particularly in times of stress. Pisces, in turn, can provide the compassion, sensitivity, and devotion that Taurus requires. Both have a love of comfort and peace, and neither is inclined toward fighting unless their ascendants fall in more aggressive signs, so they should get along well day to day. They are also capable of sparking one another's creativity and intuition, and working together to create beautiful things if they are artistically inclined.

Taurus and Pisces are also quite compatible in terms of lifestyle preferences. Both like to spend time at home and tend to prefer small gatherings of friends or family to big, wild parties. Many Tauruses and Pisceans are also drawn to the natural world and enjoy spending time outdoors in green spaces. In addition, they share a love of fine food and drink (this can be a problem as these two may encourage one another to overindulge).

Despite its many strengths, there are some potential problems with a Taurus-Pisces friendship or romantic relationship. Pisces can be inconsistent or even chaotic when under stress, which will distress stability-loving Taurus. Taurus may also resent the Piscean tendency to live in a fantasy world (or at least visit one regularly), leaving Taurus to sort out the practical issues associated with their life together. And open-minded, sensation-seeking Pisces may find Taurus overly rigid or dull at times or be put off by Taurus's acquisitive materialism. In a worst-case scenario, these two will be driven apart by their different ideals and ways of relating to the world, but in most cases, they will balance each other nicely, using their complementary strengths and abilities to support one another through hard times and build a happy life together.

Pisces + Gemini

This is a difficult combination unless other elements in their natal zodiacs are more compatible. Sensitive Pisces requires reassurance and gentleness, and Gemini is not particularly considerate or attuned to the emotional needs of others. Gemini may find Pisces needy or clingy, while Pisces finds Gemini cold and cruel. There are likely to be a lot of misunderstandings and hurt feelings with this pairing.

On the positive side, these two signs share some common ground upon which to build a relationship. Both tend to be open-minded and creative, so there is the potential to bond over shared activities. However, these signs also share some negative traits in common, including the tendency to be restless or anxious, emotionally unstable, and unrealistic about other people and the world in general. Neither sign is likely to have a particularly soothing effect on the other in day to day life; instead, they tend to stir one another up, which keeps things interesting but can also create a lot of turmoil.

To make matters worse, as a couple these two cannot compensate for each other's weaknesses because neither is pragmatic unless their ascendants fall in earth signs such as Taurus, Virgo, or Capricorn. Pisces craves security and does better with someone who can provide stability; Gemini is a maelstrom of ever-shifting feelings, preferences, and behaviors. Gemini is better able to deal with Piscean changeability than those of most other signs but may not be willing or able to support Pisces through bleak moods and periods of insecurity. Geminis tend to do better with stronger, more decisive partners because they have difficulty managing many aspects of their lives, and Pisceans want friends and partners who look after them or those they can rescue and take care of (depending on the Pisces). Independent Gemini won't play either of these roles.

Gemini and Pisces also have very different ways of relating in close relationships. Geminis tend to be direct or even blunt, though they will also dissemble to avoid trouble. Pisceans are vague, evasive, and inclined toward self-deception. Each may find the other unknowable or even untrustworthy because Gemini can't get a straight answer out of Pisces and Pisces can't get the same answer twice from Gemini. In a worst-case scenario, there will be no real communication or emotional bond between these two and their unmet needs will drive them apart. In a best-case scenario, they will bond over the common ground of curiosity, creativity, and openness to new experiences and ideas.

However, the success of this relationship will depend on the ability of Pisces to toughen up emotionally and Gemini's willingness to be more careful with Piscean feelings and provide reassurance and comfort as needed.

Pisces + Cancer

This can be a beautiful relationship, assuming that there are no serious addictions involved (both Cancer and Pisces are prone to addictive behavior). Unless their ascendants incline them toward harsher temperaments, these two water signs tend to be sensitive, compassionate, caring, creative, and idealistic. Both crave stability and substance in a relationship and both are profoundly intuitive, particularly when it comes to those they care about. A very deep emotional bond can be formed between these two signs.

Both Cancer and Pisces are highly empathic, so they'll understand one another's needs and show each other the gentleness and consideration each requires. Cancer will offer the security, stability, and protectiveness Pisces needs to feel safe, and Pisces will provide the romance and affection that Cancer requires to feel emotionally secure. Unless other elements in their natal zodiacs are highly incompatible, this should be a harmonious connection.

Despite the many strengths of this match, there are a few potential problems. Cancers tend to seek strong partners, and Pisceans are usually soft-hearted and gentle (though they may develop a tough exterior to hide this). Although Piscean gentleness is actually more compatible with Cancer's nature, some Cancers won't respect it. Also, because Cancer and Pisces are both emotionally reactive, they can be upset by even the most innocent remarks, resulting in constant emotional turmoil with a bad pairing. There are also differences in how widely these two spread their circles of compassion. Loyal Cancers tend to focus their energies on close friends and family, whereas Pisceans make no distinctions, taking in and nurturing any lost strays that come their way (which makes them vulnerable to becoming emotionally entangled with unscrupulous individuals). However, the greatest risk with this pairing is that if the Cancer-Pisces romance turns sour, these two emotionally perceptive individuals will know how to wound each other deeply. But despite these risks, the compatibility tends to be high with this match, so cruelty is less likely.

In a best-case scenario, Cancer and Pisces will have a warm, devoted, emotionally rewarding romantic relationship or friendship. They will understand each other's fluctuating moods and need for regular reassurance, and they won't be stingy about providing this support. Even if they both suffer a bleak mood at the same time, one will probably rally to support the other as both signs tend to be emotionally generous and self-sacrificing on behalf of their partners. Also, because these two individuals both tend to be creative or nature-loving (or both), they are likely to have some shared interests that will make their time together enjoyable and keep their bond strong.

Pisces + Leo

This can be a very intense and passionate combination in a romantic relationship, though these two are not particularly compatible. Leos tend to be extroverted and excitement seeking, whereas Pisceans become over-stimulated in noisy, chaotic environments. Typical Leos are relentlessly sociable, while Pisceans need plenty of time on their own to recharge their batteries, and they are likely to find the Leonine social whirlwind draining.

Leo may perceive the Piscean need spend time alone as a rejection, and Pisces may find Leo overwhelming. Each will probably seem overly needy to the other, though in different ways. Leo will have trouble coping with Pisces's dark moods, and Pisces will probably find Leo too demanding (Leos want plenty of attention and can't stand to be ignored).

Despite its shortcomings, there are some positive aspects to this pairing. A typical Pisces has no need to dominate or control others, happily letting Leo take the lead on many issues. Both signs tend to be romantic, affectionate, and idealistic, though they may also be unrealistic, putting one another up on pedestals from which they inevitably fall. Pisces will appreciate Leo's protectiveness and be impressed by Leo's self-confidence, while Leo will be intrigued by the fascinating Piscean personality. Both individuals tend to be altruistic rescuers, so they may bond over the common ground of helping other people, animals, or environmental causes. Both also tend to be creative, which provides opportunities to enjoy shared activities. However, getting along day-to-day can be difficult for this pair.

With Leo and Pisces, there tends to be a clash of preferred lifestyles. Leo wants to get out more, seeking the excitement of a crowd (and an admiring audience), whereas Pisces prefers to stick close to home or go out for a quieter activity such as a hike or dinner at a restaurant. In a romantic relationship, Pisces tends to be more open-minded and adventurous in the bedroom, whereas Leo, though passionate, is usually more conventional.

There is also a disconnect in how these two signs relate to the world. Pisces is deep, changeable, and complex, and has a tendency to withdraw when under stress to regroup and contemplate options, whereas Leo is direct, straightforward, and uncomplicated, preferring to tackle things head on and swiftly. These two may have trouble relating to one another unless other elements in their natal zodiacs bring their temperaments into closer alignment. To make matters worse, they share a penchant for self-indulgence, which means that they may bond over unhealthful pursuits such as excessive eating and or substance abuse.

Pisces + Virgo

These two signs are often drawn to one another because each has what the other lacks, and the Virgo-Pisces match can be either sheer bliss in which two people support and complete each other or a source of perpetual aggravation. There is usually no middle ground with this pairing.

Pisces and Virgo are opposite signs of the zodiac and they have very different outlooks on life, but both are self-sacrificing on behalf of others, so they tend to be very generous toward those they care about. Pisceans are naturally innovative, creative, or spiritual, which are all good complements to Virgo's rational outlook, so these two individuals can open one another's minds to new perspectives. In addition, tolerant Pisces will probably let Virgo organize their home if these two live together, which is critical to Virgo's peace of mind. On the other hand, Piscean vagueness and escapist tendencies may irritate Virgo, and Virgo's exacting and critical nature can be stressful for Pisces.

In a best-case scenario, Virgo will provide the stability and healthy environment Pisces needs, and Pisces will help Virgo open up and experience life more fully. Virgo will curb the worst Piscean excesses, and Pisces will help

Virgo loosen up and be a little decadent from time to time. However, in a worst-case scenario, Virgo will find Pisces chaotic, unstable, and deceptive (or self-deceptive), while Pisces finds Virgo cold and cruel. Much will depend on other elements in their natal zodiacs.

Virgo and Pisces usually have some common ground in terms of lifestyle preferences. Both need plenty of time alone to refresh their minds, and both thrive in calm, peaceful environments. This means that they are less likely to clash over preferred activities and overall lifestyle choices. When they do come into conflict, it's more likely to occur because Pisces perceives Virgo as harsh and distant or Virgo feels that Pisces is being impractical and unrealistic.

Because these two individuals perceive and interact with the world so differently from one another, it can be difficult for each to understand where the other is coming from, and as a result, they're likely to misinterpret one another's motives. To make this relationship work, these two will have to make an effort to understand one another's perspectives and avoid jumping to conclusions in response to statements or behaviors they don't understand. Communication and compromise will be the keys to success for this pairing.

In addition, Virgo will need to develop a softer approach to criticism, and Pisces will have to work on becoming less emotionally reactive.

Pisces + Libra

This can be a fairy-tale romance or a nightmare, but it will likely fall to one extreme or the other. Although these two signs can irritate each another, they also have plenty in common. Both tend to be romantic, creative, idealistic, aesthetically inclined, and peace seeking. Both crave harmony and avoid emotional conflict whenever possible. However, there are also some fundamental differences between these two signs that can create problems.

Pisces tends to run on intuition and emotion, while Libra favors logic and rationality. This can result in Pisces perceiving Libra as cold and only shallowly connected to others, while Libra views Pisces as irrational and emotionally draining. This pairing works best when other elements in their natal zodiacs bring their psychological styles into better alignment.

Libra and Pisces also tend to have different lifestyle preferences. Pisceans need plenty of time alone to recharge their batteries, whereas Libras want lots of time with their partners and other people. Libra's need to get out and be with others on a frequent basis may make Pisces feel insecure, while the Piscean desire for emotional reassurance may irritate Libra, who has little patience for emotional neediness.

Perhaps the most serious problem with this pairing is that both individuals tend to admire strong, decisive companions and neither can provide this for the other unless their ascendants fall in more solid signs, such as Aries, Taurus, Leo, Scorpio, or Capricorn. Each may look to the other to take the lead in a crisis situation and neither may volunteer.

Despite the problems with this pairing, it does have some strengths. Both signs need a peaceful home life to be mentally healthy, and both are inclined to compromise and try to understand the perspectives of others rather than demanding that others convert to their own points of view. This increases the likelihood that these two can live together without major clashes. They are also inclined to find one another's minds interesting, so they are unlikely to grow bored with each other. If other elements in their natal zodiacs are compatible, this match has potential.

Pisces + Scorpio

This is a great match unless other elements in their natal zodiacs are highly incompatible. The mutual sympathy between these two signs enables them to develop a very powerful bond.

Scorpio and Pisces can intuit each other's feelings and provide the emotional support each requires. In romance, the passion is strong with this pairing. However, this connection tends to be so intense that one unstable partner can easily destabilize the other.

Scorpio and Pisces have much in common, but they also have a number of complementary traits that increase the likelihood of success for both friendships and romantic partnerships. Pisces will appreciate Scorpio's strength, particularly during stressful times when a good, solid anchor is needed. Scorpio stays cool in a crisis, which is a trait that Pisces values. Pisces, in turn, fascinates Scorpio and stimulates Scorpio's creative energies. Pisceans have profound thoughts and feelings, which is important to this match because Scorpios loathe shallowness. In romance, this tends to be an exciting and highly compatible pairing, but it also works well in friendship because these two tend to bring out the best in each other.

Pisces is emotionally gentle, and therefore less likely to hurt Scorpio's feelings. Scorpio is inclined to lash out when hurt, which can irreparably damage a relationship with a Pisces, but Pisces doesn't usually provoke this sort of response (the exception to this rule is a Pisces with a combative rising sign such as Aries, Leo, or Sagittarius). Both Scorpio and Pisces are typically compassionate and self-sacrificing, so they are inclined to show one another kindness as required, even in difficult situations. These two are unlikely to abandon one another in a crisis, but instead show their best sides when needed by each other. Both tend to devote themselves fully to their relationships and form intense connections, so this pairing is more likely to stick than many others.

Lifestyle preferences are usually well-matched with this pair. Both signs tend toward introversion (unless their ascendants fall in more gregarious signs), and after a period of socializing, they need to spend time on their own or alone with their partners. Both require solitary, safe places where they can retreat as needed, and both usually have solo hobbies. These two individuals will often be content to spend quiet time together, pursuing their own separate interests in the same place, enjoying one another's presence without needing to interact continuously, so they can be good roommates as well as good friends or romantic partners.

Pisces + Sagittarius

These two signs are often drawn together, yet they are not particularly compatible unless other elements in their natal zodiacs bring their temperaments into better alignment. Pisces tends to be sensitive and Sagittarius is naturally insensitive (the exception to this rule is a Sagittarius with a water rising sign – Cancer, Scorpio, or Pisces). Tactless Sagittarius can inflict deep wounds without meaning to, and reactive Pisces may become deceptive, evasive, or escapist if the relationship sours. Sagittarians tend to address problems in a forthright way even when tact is called for, whereas Pisceans will dissemble to keep the peace, so their communication styles are incompatible. These two signs also tend to look for different things in a romantic partner. Pisces wants a stable anchor, a fantasy lover, or someone to rescue or be rescued by, while Sagittarius wants a buddy with whom to share adventures.

Sagittarius and Pisces tend to have a destabilizing effect on one another. Sagittarius is likely to drag Pisces out into a whirlwind of relentless socializing and other activity that leaves Pisces feeling drained and emotionally ravaged, or Pisces may pull Sagittarius into a solitary world of emotional chaos. These two can also have difficulty providing the support each needs in times of stress. Pisces requires reassurance, stability, and gentle treatment when under pressure, but Sagittarius craves action and change in times of adversity (and prefers a partner who grants the freedom to pursue them).

Sagittarius and Pisces can also bring out the worst in each other due to the few traits they share. Both are dreamers and sensation seekers who try to cast off life's limitations. Together, they may encourage one another's tendencies toward excessive spending, eating, substance abuse, or risking everything on grandiose dreams.

On the plus side, these two individuals do have some traits that appeal to each another. Sagittarius is drawn to the mysterious, intriguing Pisces mind, while Pisces can be uplifted by Sagittarius's vigorous energy, confidence, and sunny optimism. Both tend to be generous, open-minded, and altruistic, and both have a desire to do something positive in the world to help humanity, animals, or the environment, so they may bond over the common ground of volunteer work or participation in sociopolitical causes. However, although these two may be powerfully attracted to one another and find each other's minds fascinating, they will probably have difficulty living together unless other elements in their natal zodiacs are more harmonious and stabilizing.

Pisces + Capricorn

This can be a very deep and powerful connection, most often beautiful, though occasionally ugly. Capricorn might not like the Piscean tendencies toward escapism and daydreaming, and Pisces may find Capricorn too harsh and exacting, but overall, despite the fact that they have fundamentally different natures, these two are quite well-suited to each other.

Pisces and Capricorn perceive the world in very different ways. Pisceans are open-minded, trusting (and somewhat gullible), creative, intuitive, and sensitive, whereas Capricorns tend to be skeptical, distrustful (until they know someone well), rational, materialistic, and pragmatic. In a best-case scenario, these two will adopt some of each other's more positive traits so that Pisces becomes more discerning and pragmatic and Capricorn grows more open-minded and willing to give others the benefit of the doubt when the situation warrants it.

These two form a nice complement to one another in many ways. Pisces creates an atmosphere of love and compassion in which Capricorn can open up and feel safe, while Capricorn provides the stability that Pisces desperately needs. Piscean warmth can melt the cool

Capricorn exterior, while Capricorn's strength and commitment help Pisces feel safe and secure. Capricorn needs admiration to feel loved, and Pisces can offer this psychological support. Capricorn, in turn, has the maturity and self-discipline required to take care of a partner, which provides a much-needed safety net for Pisces. Capricorn can also improve Pisces's physical health by encouraging a more active lifestyle and discouraging addictive tendencies, and Pisces can improve Capricorn's mental health by encouraging a more positive outlook on life.

Both signs require a quiet, peaceful, stable home and they will probably want to spend a lot of time there unless other elements in their natal zodiacs incline them toward roaming. Pisces may live in a state of chaos with items piled high in closets, exploding from drawers, or even strewn across the floor, while Capricorn requires order and tidiness, so when these two live together, there may be some friction regarding housekeeping. However, in terms of overall lifestyle, Capricorn and Pisces tend to be quite compatible. Both are typically somewhat introverted, so they will respect one another's need for time alone to pursue solitary interests, and they are inclined to enjoy each other's company when the two of them spend time alone together.

Pisces + Aquarius

This match can go either way. On one hand, the Piscean's eccentric, original (and in some cases, bohemian) style appeals to Aquarius, and Pisces is fascinated by the Aquarian's unconventionality and innovativeness. Both Aquarius and Pisces tend to see the world in grand, sweeping terms. They are idealistic sensation-seekers, so neither can act as an anchor for the other. This combination ensures a very interesting meeting of the minds, but there are a number of significant differences in how these two signs interact with the world that can create problems in a serious relationship.

Although both have a tendency toward altruism, Pisces is typically the more compassionate of the two. Aquarius has humanitarian ideals but thinks in terms of changing the world to make it better for many people (or all of them) rather than ministering to the emotional needs of individuals.

Pisceans are also very sensitive, both to the feelings of others and on their own behalf. Pisces is easily hurt by careless statements, which emotionally oblivious Aquarius is prone to making, so there is the potential for emotional damage here. On the other hand, both signs tend to be tolerant and nonjudgmental, which reduces the risk of conflicts and allows both members of this pair to be themselves without fear of censure.

Another problem with this combination is that Aquarius needs a lot of personal freedom, whereas Pisces requires plenty of reassurance (and comforting when bleak moods strike). Aquarius may find Pisces needy or overly emotional (which will send Aquarius packing), and Pisces may find Aquarius devastatingly cold and distant (which will send Pisces off in search of a more sympathetic partner). Aquarians tend to spread their energies among many different people, treating friends and lovers similarly, but Pisceans need to feel that they are being prioritized by their partners.

Another potential problem is that Pisceans want to rescue someone else or be rescued (depending on other personality factors) and independent Aquarius is not inclined to fulfill either of these roles, so Pisces may wander off in search of someone who is more needy or has a desire to take care of others. To make matters worse, neither sign tends to be particularly stable in terms of emotions or lifestyle, so they can't provide stability for one other unless their ascendants fall in more solid signs such as Taurus, Cancer, Leo, Scorpio, or Capricorn.

In a best-case scenario, these two will learn from each other. Pisces would benefit from developing some emotional detachment and a thicker skin, and Aquarius could benefit from cultivating Piscean strengths such as intuition and sensitivity to the feelings of others. Both individuals are prone to streaks of brilliance, so their intellectual rapport can lead to the generation of fascinating new ideas and insights, and if they work together, they can harness great collective potential for creativity and innovation. However, although this match does have some positive elements, these two will need to compromise on a number of issues.

Aquarius will have to provide more affection and reassurance than is typical for this sign, as well as showing more restraint when broaching sensitive issues, and Pisces will need to let Aquarius pursue friendships and activities outside the primary relationship.

Pisces + Pisces

This can be a beautiful combination. When two Pisceans get together, their connection tends to be deep, profound, and harmonious. There is a risk that these two individuals will feed one another's addictive, self-indulgent, or self-destructive tendencies, or they could become so involved with one another that they shut out the rest of the world, departing from the collective reality to create their own personal magical universe. However, assuming that neither individual has serious problems with addiction or mental illness, two Pisceans should be highly compatible, mutually compassionate, attuned to each other's needs, and accepting of one another as they are.

A pair of Pisceans should get along well if they decide to live together because their lifestyle preferences will be similar. Both need time alone to recharge after periods of socializing, so they will understand this tendency in one another, and both like to spend time at home. Pisceans don't need to chatter at one another continuously. Instead, they can simply enjoy each other's company even when pursuing their own hobbies and interests side by side or in different rooms. Pisceans need a peaceful, calm home where they can retreat from the noise and chaos of the world outside, so they are likely to keep their living space serene and comfortable.

Problems may arise with the Pisces-Pisces pairing if either (or both) partners or friends have troubles with addiction. Neither will be inclined to restrain the other; instead, they are likely to act as enablers, making the problem worse. Pisceans are tolerant live-and-let-live types, which is a good thing in most cases, but when it comes to self-destructive behavior in others, they are less inclined to put a stop to it. Pisceans are also quite sensitive, so if these two do fight, neither is likely to get over it quickly or easily. Fortunately, this pair is more inclined to avoid conflict than to provoke it.

When two artistic or innovative Pisceans get together, they can really have a blast. These imaginative individuals fuel one another's creative energies and they can come up with ground-breaking new ideas or create beautiful things. However, even if they don't share one another's interests, Pisceans don't demand that their partners or friends take up their preferred hobbies. As long as they feel that the relationship is solid and secure, they are happy to support the interests of others, even to the point of self-sacrifice at times. They are also inclined to keep their mouths shut when they disapprove of anything, which reduces the likelihood of nasty fights. Overall, this is a good match unless other elements in their natal zodiacs are highly incompatible.

Chapter 4: Pisces Love and Marriage

Traditional astrological wisdom holds that Pisceans are most compatible with Taurus, Cancer, Scorpio, Capricorn, and Pisces, and least compatible with Aries, Gemini, Leo, Virgo, Libra, and Sagittarius. But what do the actual marriage and divorce statistics say?

Mathematician Gunter Sachs (1998) conducted a large-scale study of sun signs, encompassing nearly one million people in Switzerland, which found statistically significant results on a number of measures including marriage and divorce. Castille (2000) conducted a similar study in France using marriage statistics collected between 1976 and 1997, which included more than six million marriages.

Based on the findings of these studies, marriage pairings are ranked from most to least frequent on the pages that follow (* indicates that the result is statistically significant – in other words, the marriage rate was much higher or lower than would occur by chance).

Sachs also gathered divorce statistics, but Pisceans were not more likely to divorce any particular sign, though Pisces women were less likely to divorce Capricorn men than men of any other sign, and Pisces men were least likely to divorce Scorpio women.

Pisces Men

Sachs Study

1. Scorpio*
2. Aquarius
3. Aries
4. Taurus
5. Cancer
6. Pisces (same rate as Sagittarius)
7. Sagittarius
8. Gemini
9. Leo
10. Capricorn
11. Libra*
12. Virgo*

Castille Study

1. Pisces*
2. Aries
3. Scorpio
4. Virgo
5. Leo
6. Sagittarius
7. Taurus
8. Aquarius
9. Capricorn
10. Gemini
11. Libra*
12. Cancer*

Pisces Women

Sachs Study

1. Scorpio*
2. Cancer
3. Capricorn
4. Aries
5. Leo
6. Aquarius
7. Pisces
8. Gemini
9. Libra
10. Virgo
11. Taurus
12. Sagittarius*

Castille Study

1. Pisces*
2. Taurus
3. Aquarius
4. Aries
5. Scorpio
6. Leo
7. Libra
8. Capricorn
9. Cancer
10. Virgo
11. Sagittarius*
12. Gemini

Some Notes on Marriage Rates

Sachs found that Pisces men most frequently married and were least likely to divorce Scorpio women. Pisces women were also most likely to marry Scorpio men and least likely to divorce Capricorns, according to the Sachs study findings, whereas Castille found that both Pisces men and women were most likely to marry other Pisceans.

It's no surprise to see Scorpio topping the marriage list for Pisces. These two signs are considered highly compatible by traditional astrologers. Both are water signs, and therefore inclined to be sensitive, compassionate, emotionally intense, and introverted.

Even in the areas where the two signs differ, they bring complementary strengths to a relationship. Scorpios offer the stability Pisceans need, and Pisceans have an intuitive sense of what to say and do to help Scorpios relax and learn to trust.

With two such deep, intuitive signs, there is the potential for an exceptionally profound connection. Piscean openness helps to break down the fierce emotional defenses Scorpio maintains, while Scorpio provides the support required to help Pisces stay balanced and on track.

The popularity of the Pisces-Pisces match is also unsurprising. Two Pisceans will understand each other on a deep level, and they are likely to have similar lifestyle, relationship, and social preferences. Neither will pressure the other to do social things when their partners are in introvert mode, and they are likely to share hobbies and interests in common. Moreover, even when they pursue different interests, they can enjoy doing their own things in the same home, completely absorbed in their individual activities, but comforted by the awareness of each other's presence.

Sachs also found that Pisces women were least likely to divorce Capricorns. The Pisces-Capricorn match may be favored due to their complementary traits. Pisces can encourage cautious Capricorn to open up and trust, while Capricorn can make Pisces feel secure, and both signs tend to be careful with money, so fights over finances are less likely. Both signs also tend to be introverted and enjoy spending their free time pursuing hobbies rather than going out on the town, so their lifestyle preferences tend to be compatible.

The finding that Pisces men are less inclined to marry Virgos and Libras is also in keeping with conventional astrological wisdom. Emotionally guarded, intellectually oriented, rational Virgo doesn't always make an easy match with sensitive, affectionate, open-minded Pisces. As for Libra, Pisceans need a lot of alone time to recharge, which may not appeal to sociable Libras, who like to go out and meet new people on a regular basis. Also, Libras tend to evaluate conflicts in a rational, detached manner, whereas Pisceans will passionately defend a particular side (usually that of the underdog) if they believe someone has been mistreated, so the two may come into conflict over people-related issues.

Finding Cancer at the bottom of the Pisces men's marriage list in the Castille study is surprising. According to traditional astrological wisdom, these signs should be highly compatible, though perhaps the compatibility level is so high that these two individuals more often end up as friends than lovers. Or Cancer moodiness combined with Piscean sensitivity may be a volatile mix for some couples (it might be problematic to have two emotionally reactive people in a relationship).

Sachs also found that Pisces women were less likely to marry Sagittarians than those of any other sign, and

Castille found that Pisces women married Sagittarians less frequently than any other sign except Gemini. These are expected results, given the fundamental incompatibilities between the two signs.

Pisces needs reassurance and comfort during bleak moods, whereas Sagittarius, though generous with time and money, tend to be insensitive. Sagittarian tactlessness and bluntness can be devastating for Pisces, and independent Sagittarians may find Pisceans too intense or needy when they're working their way through dark emotional states. Pisceans are likely to find Sagittarians an unreliable source of emotional support, and to make matters worse, Sagittarian carelessness with money can be stressful for more fiscally cautious Pisceans. However, although this match can be challenging, the prospects are far better for this pairing if the two individuals have highly compatible rising signs or moon signs.

The Castille study found that Piscean women were less likely to marry Gemini men than men of any other sun sign. This is an expected result as well because these two signs are also considered fundamentally incompatible by traditional astrologers.

Pisces is a sign of depths and extremes, which creates a need for consistency and stability in a partner, and Gemini is erratic, flitting from one thing to the next and having difficulty settling on any one place, belief system, job, set of activities, or overall lifestyle.

Pisces women are also happier with partners who provide reliable emotional support, and Geminis do not make good emotional anchors with their constant changes of mood and preference. However, if the rising signs or moon signs of the two individuals are more compatible, these difficulties can be diminished.

The Best Romantic Match for Pisces

The best match for Pisces is often another Pisces or a Scorpio. Two Pisceans are fundamentally compatible in terms of lifestyle preferences and emotional styles, whereas Pisces and Scorpio bring complementary strengths to a marriage and tend to bring out the best in each other. Pisceans can help Scorpios relax and lower their emotional barriers, and Scorpios can keep Pisceans grounded and stabilized and make them feel protected and loved.

Although Pisces and Scorpio tend to be particularly compatible matches for Pisceans, those who find themselves romantically entangled with one of the less compatible signs should not despair. Plenty of marriages between supposedly incompatible signs have lasted.

It's important to keep in mind that these are statistical tendencies; this doesn't mean that every romance between incompatible signs is doomed. For example, out of 6,498,320 marriages encompassing all possible sign combinations in the Castille study, there were 1,323 *more* marriages between Pisces men and Pisces women than would be expected if sun signs had no effect, whereas between Pisces men and Cancer women, there were 474 *fewer* marriages than would be expected if pairings were random. However, there still were many marriages between the supposedly least compatible signs.

Astrology is complex, and there is more to consider than just sun signs. Two people with incompatible sun signs may have highly compatible rising signs or moon signs that can make the difference between a bad match and a good match with a bit of an "edge" that keeps things interesting.

*The Sachs study has been criticized for not taking potential confounding variables into account and continues to be controversial. I have found no critiques of the Castille study thus far.

Chapter 5: Why Some Signs Are More Compatible With Pisces Than Others

Why are some astrological signs considered more or less compatible with Pisces than others? Traditional astrologers believe that signs of the same element will be the most compatible, and that fire and air signs will be more compatible with one another, as will earth and water signs, whereas fire and air are more likely to clash with earth and water. They also believe that clashes are more likely to occur among different signs of the same quality (cardinal, fixed, or mutable).

Compatibility according to traditional astrologers:

- Pisces (water, mutable) + Aries (fire, cardinal): somewhat challenging

- Pisces (water, mutable) + Taurus (earth, fixed): good

- Pisces (water, mutable) + Gemini (air, mutable): very challenging

- Pisces (water, mutable) + Cancer (water, cardinal): excellent

- Pisces (water, mutable) + Leo (fire, fixed): somewhat challenging

- Pisces (water, mutable) + Virgo (earth, mutable): very challenging

- Pisces (water, mutable) + Libra (air, cardinal): somewhat challenging

- Pisces (water, mutable) + Scorpio (water, fixed): excellent

- Pisces (water, mutable) + Sagittarius (fire, mutable): very challenging

- Pisces (water, mutable) + Capricorn (earth, cardinal): good

- Pisces (water, mutable) + Aquarius (air, fixed): somewhat challenging

- Pisces (water, mutable) + Pisces (water, mutable): excellent

Note: Two people who seem incompatible based on their sun signs may actually be far more compatible than expected because the elements and qualities of other placements in their natal zodiacs (ascendants, moon signs, etc.) are a much better match. See Appendix 2 for more information on this.

The Elements

The astrological elements are fire, earth, air, and water. Each element includes three of the twelve astrological signs.

Fire Signs: Aries, Leo, Sagittarius

Those who have a lot of planets in fire signs tend to be courageous, enterprising, and confident. Their love of excitement causes them take risks, and they are often extravagant or careless with money.

Fire people are generous to a fault, idealistic, and helpful. They are quick to anger, but also quick to forgive, and usually honest, in many cases to the point of bluntness or tactlessness.

Fire people are energetic and often athletic. They are assertive and (in some cases) aggressive or argumentative. Impulsivity can lead to poor decisions, financial disasters, and unnecessary conflict. Extroverted and easily bored, they seek attention and tend to be affectionate and friendly.

Earth Signs: Taurus, Virgo, Capricorn

Those who have many planets in earth signs tend to be responsible, reliable, and trustworthy. They can usually be counted on to provide stability and practical help, and they are loyal to their friends and not inclined to be fickle, though when someone crosses them, they can be quite ruthless in cutting that person out of their lives forever. Slow to anger but equally slow to forgive, they often hold grudges. However, they are usually reasonable and diplomatic unless severely provoked.

People whose natal zodiacs are weighted toward earth signs tend to be physically strong and have great endurance. They are inclined to achieve success through hard work, and their innate cautiousness, fear of change, and need for security keep them from making rash decisions or gambling excessively, though these traits can also cause them to miss opportunities or get into ruts. While not exceptionally innovative, they have good follow-through and are able to finish what they start.

Air Signs: Gemini, Libra, Aquarius

Those who have a lot of planets in air signs are intellectual rather than emotional, which can cause some to view them as insensitive, though they tend to be friendly and sociable. Logical, rational, and emotionally detached by nature, they can be open-minded and non-judgmental in most cases.

People whose natal zodiacs are weighted toward air signs are adaptable, mentally flexible, and easy going. They rarely blow up at others in anger-provoking situations, as they are more inclined to analyze circumstances than to react passionately. They are also easily bored and require a diverse array of social companions, hobbies, and other entertainments.

Air people usually love change and tend to be experimental and open to new experiences. Impulsivity and curiosity can cause them to make impractical decisions or squander their money.

Water Signs: Cancer, Scorpio, Pisces

Those who have many planets in water signs are highly intuitive, which enables them to discern the emotions, needs, and motivations of others. They are compassionate and inclined to care for the physically sick and the emotionally damaged, self-sacrificing on behalf of those they care for, and even in the service of strangers in some cases.

Sensitive and easily hurt, many water people develop a tough outer shell to hide their vulnerability. They are passionate in their attachments to people and prone to jealousy. Because they are idealistic, they often gloss over the faults of others, so they can be deceived by unscrupulous people.

Water people are sensual and creative. Given the right environment and opportunity, they can produce art, music, literature, or in some cases, inventions or scientific ideas that have profound effects on others.

The Qualities

The astrological qualities are fixed, cardinal, and mutable. Each category includes four of the astrological signs.

Cardinal: Aries, Cancer, Libra, Capricorn

A person with the majority of natal planets in cardinal signs will be enterprising and inclined to initiate courses of action. Cardinal people make things happen and transform situations. This can be done for the benefit or detriment of others.

Fixed: Taurus, Leo, Scorpio, Aquarius

Those who have a lot of planets in fixed signs have good follow-through. They tend to stick to a single course of action and carry out activities to their completion or conclusion. Fixed-sign people are often moody or stubborn, and they have intense reactions to things. However, they can act as stabilizing forces for others because they tend to behave in a consistent manner.

Mutable: Gemini, Virgo, Sagittarius, Pisces

Those who have the majority of their planets in mutable signs are flexible and adaptable. They accept change and adjust well to new circumstances that can throw other types off kilter. Mutable people often function better in a crisis than in a stable situation.

Chapter 6: Pisces Children

Pisces children are usually sweet, kind-hearted, affectionate, creative, artistic, innovative, and (in many cases) musically gifted. They are often brilliant in at least one area, and when provided with the supplies required to develop their talents, they can become outstanding in their preferred activities.

Pisces children are incredibly sensitive, not only on their own behalf, but also to the feelings of others. They are also highly imaginative and intuitive, which increases the likelihood that they will have strange experiences, such as seeing ghosts. They are very sensitive to environments and may be upset by things that others can't perceive, and some have an eerie ability to express a thought that a nearby adult is trying to hide.

Pisces children often have vivid dreams, and many suffer from bizarre nightmares. They are also inclined to daydream or find other means of escape when things get stressful or boring.

Many Pisces children spend a lot of time engaging in artistic pursuits, building things with blocks or craft materials, or wandering around in a fantasy world. They tend to be forgetful when it comes to chores or other required activities, but they are rarely, if ever, mean or aggressive without serious provocation.

Pisces children will never forget a cruel word and they are easily psychologically damaged, so it is important to treat them gently. They are compassionate toward others and usually develop a social conscience and a desire to help those in need at a very young age.

Because they are naturally empathic, Pisces children may bring home stray animals or even kids who have bad home lives (or pretend that they do). Pisces children are naïve and trusting, so they easily deceived despite their intelligence. They can be led astray, and in adolescence they are particularly vulnerable to abusing alcohol and drugs or being abused by unscrupulous peers or adults.

Typical Pisces children are sympathetic, compassionate, tolerant, and willing to do almost anything to avoid confrontation, even if this means being evasive or lying outright. However, they use their incredible imaginations to convince themselves that their lies are actually truths as they speak them, so they are not really lying to others, but instead deceiving themselves (some Pisceans maintain this tendency into adulthood).

In addition to arts, crafts, and scientific pursuits, many Pisceans show an affinity for water activities as children and should ideally have swimming lessons at a young age. Being in or near water is a good stress reliever for Piscean children (and adults).

Dancing, singing, martial arts, or music lessons can also be beneficial for developing confidence and reducing anxiety, and many Piscean children have natural aptitudes for one or more of these activities. However, the benefits only occur if the child actually chooses and enjoys the activity. Pisces children who are forced into activities they dislike tend to suffer more intense stress reactions than children of other signs, which can lead to anxiety or depression.

Chapter 7: Pisces Parents

Typical Pisces parents are gentle and kind, not prone to engaging in screaming arguments or humiliating their children in public with dramatic displays of emotion or disapproval.

When Pisces parents argue with their spouses, they try to keep it low-key so as not to distress their children, and because they are not very argumentative by nature, ferocious fights are rare to nonexistent.

On those rare occasions when they are very angry with their partners or children, Pisces parents are more likely to engage in passive aggression (nagging or a barrier of silence) rather than overt hostility, so their children are less likely to be traumatized by household violence (unless the Pisces parent has a more aggressive rising sign).

Pisceans can sublimate their own needs to take care of others, particularly those who are sick or suffering, which is among their great strengths as parents. They set a good example by being kind and helpful toward others as well as their own children, though in some cases they go overboard, taking in every human and animal stray they come across or squandering large amounts of time and energy in the service of selfish individuals with convincing sob stories.

Pisceans hate letting others down so they find it difficult to say "no". Pisces parents have a tendency to take on more than they should and sometimes feel resentful later on, leading to a passive-aggressive martyr complex. A major challenge for this sign is developing a healthy level of assertiveness to avoid becoming overburdened by others.

Pisces parents tend to interact with their children in original and, in some cases, unpredictable ways, and many favor extreme parenting styles. Some are so anxious and overprotective that their children become equally fearful or, if they're bolder by nature, sneak out to do their own thing without parental oversight. Other Pisceans are so lax, permissive, or caught up in their own personal lives that their children run wild without boundaries. Pisces parents may swing from one extreme to the other when it comes to different issues; it is hard for them to do anything in moderation or with any consistency, and their changes of mood and parenting approaches can be disconcerting for their children. However, these Piscean extremes usually arise from good intentions: overprotective parents want to keep their kids safe and healthy, while permissive parents want them to be free, independent, and happy.

The sign of Pisces is associated with unconditional love, and Pisceans can forgive their children anything. This sign is also known for intuition, and Pisces parents often have an intuitive link with their kids and other family members that alerts them when something is wrong.

Parenthood can be challenging for Pisceans because they desperately need to be alone at times and this is difficult with children around. Some may find ways to retreat or escape: television, books, alcohol, walking, running, or other solitary pursuits. In a worst-case scenario, the Piscean parent will escape into a self-absorbed fantasy world or a more exciting relationship, emotionally or physically abandoning the family. However, most are devoted to their children to the point where they sacrifice their own emotional needs to prioritize those of their loved ones.

Pisces parents should take some time for themselves on a regular basis to engage in hobbies or other activities on their own. After refreshing themselves through solitude, they have more energy for others.

Pisces parents usually have an interest in one or more of the pastimes associated with this sign, which include photography, film, science, art, and nature, and they often share these interests in their children. Creative, scientific, and nature-based activities can provide a basis for parent-child bonding time, as introverted Pisceans tend to prefer interacting while doing something constructive or immersive rather than just sitting around and talking.

Chapter 8: Pisces Health

Pisceans often suffer from extreme fluctuations of mood and emotion, and their tendency to worry and obsess over things can lead to depression or anxiety disorders.

Because Pisceans pick up on the moods and emotions of others, it is important for them to spend time with positive people who encourage an optimistic outlook on life. They also need to spend time alone after periods of sociability because if they don't get this time to recharge, they can become distressed or emotionally and physically exhausted.

Pisces is an addictive sign, particularly prone to alcoholism, so Pisceans must learn to curb their escapist tendencies, or addiction can lead to health problems.

Pisceans are also so open-minded and imaginative that they can lose touch with reality altogether. Spaciness, forgetfulness, and even insanity are linked with the sign of Pisces, though serious mental health problems usually result from addictions or extreme stress rather than an innate tendency to go off the rails (Pisceans who maintain healthy lifestyles and spend time with good people are far less likely to have problems).

Addiction to food is also a common problem for Pisceans, leading to obesity and related health issues, so they must be careful not to engage in mindless or comfort eating.

Traditional astrologers believe that Pisceans are prone to lymphatic, hormonal, and glandular disorders, as well as headaches, foot problems, and allergies to particular ingredients or food additives and preservatives, and to cleaning and industrial chemicals. They are also vulnerable to experiencing strange, hard-to-diagnose symptoms when under stress that go away once the stressful situation is over.

Eating clean, whole foods and using natural cleaning products can reduce the likelihood of problems for Pisceans, and certain physical activities are particularly beneficial as well.

Swimming, martial arts, dance, and yoga can help Pisceans maintain the mind-body balance required for mental and physical health, and spending time near water tends to have a powerful calming and healing effect as well.

Pisceans are also great visualizers, so they can benefit from complementary visualization therapies that trigger the body's own healing mechanisms when used in conjunction with regular medical treatments.

Chapter 9: Pisces Hobbies

Pastimes associated with the sign of Pisces include:

- arts and crafts (especially painting)
- baths
- boating
- caring for pets or plants
- collecting beautiful things
- dancing
- daydreaming
- gardening
- listening to or making music
- martial arts
- occult, paranormal, or mystical studies

- photography
- reading
- scientific studies
- singing
- spiritual pursuits
- sunbathing
- swimming
- video games
- visiting galleries and museums
- volunteer work
- walking/hiking
- watching movies or television
- writing

Chapter 10: Pisces Careers

Many Pisceans have trouble maintaining ordinary nine-to-five routines, which can lead to unemployment for some. The majority do best in artistic, nurturing, or scientific work—anything that requires inspiration or creativity.

When they do find their niches, Pisceans are dedicated to their professions. This is a self-sacrificing sign, and

Pisceans can work tirelessly on behalf of others in charitable, healing, compassionate, or scientific occupations. They are happiest when they are needed, and when they have opportunities to improve the lives of others, which can lead them into medical, nursing, caretaking, and animal rescue fields, or to the furthering of scientific knowledge.

Pisceans are extremely sensitive to atmospheres, so a negative work environment can cause health problems. They also need time alone, so they are better suited to occupations that allow for some solitary time unless their ascendants incline them to be more extroverted than typical Pisceans.

Pisces Occupations

Pisces careers and career fields, according to traditional astrologers, include:

- actor/actress
- animal rescue worker
- any job with boats
- artist (especially painter or sculptor)
- chiropodist/ podiatrist
- counselor
- dancer
- doctor
- engineer

- fiction writer/poet
- film industry worker
- home care worker
- inventor
- institutional worker (especially in prisons or mental health facilities)
- lab technician
- marine biologist
- massage therapist/ physiotherapist
- naturopath
- nurse
- oceanographer
- photographer
- priest
- psychic
- reflexologist
- scientist
- singer
- swimming instructor

Note: The sun sign is only one aspect of an astrological profile. Many other factors play a role, including rising and moon signs. For example, a person with the sun in Pisces and Aries rising may be more inclined to choose a career such as firefighter that involves both danger and selflessness, rather than one of the less risky Piscean careers, and a Pisces with Leo rising would be drawn to the more sociable professions on the Pisces list. Learning about additional astrological placements provides more comprehensive insights into potential career aptitudes.

Chapter 11: Pisces Differences

Sachs collected a large volume of market research data for his study, and this data showed some average differences among the sun signs for certain beliefs, attitudes, interests, hobbies, activities, and preferences. The following are items for which there was a significant difference between Pisces and the sun sign average (a significantly higher or lower percentage of positive or negative responses from Pisceans compared to the average for all the sun signs). Not all Pisceans followed these trends; they were just more likely to match them than those of other sun signs.

Environmental Conservation

Pisceans were more likely to be interested in environmental protection and nature conservation. This is an expected finding, given that Pisces is known as a nature-loving sign.

Responsibility

Pisceans were more likely to say that they like taking on responsibility. This goes against traditional astrological characterizations of Pisces as insecure or dependent. However, because Pisceans run to extremes, although some may be very dependent, others will be unusually responsible and capable.

Interests

Pisceans were more likely to give advice on further professional training, building and renovation, gardening and garden layout, and catering for guests or hospitality, all of which are in keeping with traditional views of the Pisces persona.

Professional Training

Pisceans were more likely to say they were interested in further professional training. This is no surprise, as training can provide a means to financial and career security.

Building and Renovation

Pisceans were also more likely to express an interest in building and renovation, which is also unsurprising because building and renovation satisfy the Piscean desires for security, aesthetically pleasing surroundings, and opportunities to create new things.

Gardening

Pisceans were more likely to express an interest in gardening, probably because its solitary nature is appealing to introverts, and it provides time out in nature, which has a positive effect on mood and overall mental health. Pisceans tend to be talented in the areas of decoration and design, and gardening allows them to apply these talents to the development of beautiful outdoor spaces.

Entertaining

Pisceans were also more likely to express an interest in entertaining, which is unsurprising because they enjoy good food and drink and their generous natures make them want to share these things. They love taking care of others and making them happy and entertaining a small group of friends or family members in a comfortable, familiar environment is an ideal way for Pisceans to socialize, as it avoids the harsher elements of many social venues (noise, crowds, etc.) that most Pisceans find stressful.

Clothing Preferences

Pisceans were more likely to choose comfortable clothing (as opposed to fashionable, trendy, sporty, etc.). They were also more likely to prefer clothing that could be described as practical or suitable rather than extravagant, vivid, or tight.

Pisces is a comfort-loving sign, so the preference for comfortable clothing would be expected. Also, Pisceans are not slaves to fashion; most do not follow trends or do things just because other people think they should do them, so they are less likely to be swayed by the whims of social preference for particular types of clothing (unless soft, comfortable, functional, loose, or stretchy clothing is currently in fashion).

Marriage

Pisces men were more likely to say that they were eager to get married, and they were less likely to be single. Pisceans tend to be happier in partnerships, so this is unsurprising, as is the fact that Pisces men were more likely to be married because this sign tends to be intriguing and attractive to others. Also, Pisceans are usually open-minded in their search for a partner, finding many different qualities attractive rather than fixating on a narrow type, which increases their likelihood of finding a good match.

Entertainments

Pisceans were more likely than those of other signs to listen to folk music and watch or listen to one to three hours of television, video, or radio in their leisure time. This is also in keeping with the escapist Piscean nature, and the sign's love of fantasy worlds and music.

Holidays

Pisceans were more likely to be the sole decision makers when it came to making holiday plans. This is also an expected finding, as they tend to have strong, intuitive feelings about places that draw them powerfully to certain destinations or accommodations while making others repellant. Typical Pisceans also prefer to avoid noisy, crowded, chaotic places, so they may take charge of the decision-making process to avoid stressful destinations.

Pisceans were also more inclined than those of other signs to take short holiday trips, in keeping with the escapist nature of this sign (but also the tendency to seek comfort and stability, as they liked to get away but also to come home soon afterward).

Purchases

Pisceans were more likely to own prints, paintings, and sculptures; diesel, battery, or electric lawnmowers; and cars.

Prints and paintings are associated with the sign of Pisces and many Pisceans have an interest in gardening, so these findings are also in accordance with the traditional astrological view of this sign.

The love of cars also makes sense because Pisceans appreciate beautiful things, seek a means of escape from difficult situations (which cars provide), are soothed by motion when under stress, and prefer comfortable environments when traveling.

Higher Education

Sachs found that Pisceans were more likely to study psychology and less likely to study veterinary medicine than those of other signs.

Psychology is considered a typical Piscean interest by traditional astrologers, given the sign's association with depths, secrets, healing, and the intangible aspects of life.

Pisceans may be less inclined to study veterinary medicine because they are particularly sensitive to the suffering others and may have trouble euthanizing animals or seeing them in pain.

Jobs

Sachs found that Pisceans were less likely than those of other signs to be in executive positions. This is not surprising, given that Pisceans are usually introverted and not inclined toward self-promotion (unless they have fire ascendants such as Aries, Leo, or Sagittarius, or air ascendants such as Gemini, Libra, or Aquarius).

Pisceans were more likely to be farmers, carpenters, mechanical engineers, nurses, further education teachers, primary school teachers, and kindergarten teachers, and less likely to be bakers, painters, furniture makers, bank clerks, hairdressers, or chemists.

Farming provides opportunities to work with plants and animals and spend plenty of time alone while having control of the workflow and workspace, which would be very appealing to typical Pisceans.

Carpentry and mechanical engineering are also good careers for those who need time alone, as these fields provide opportunities to either engage in solitary work or work quietly with a small group. Also, many Pisceans like to build and engineer things, and these jobs provide opportunities to be creative.

Teaching is a relatively secure profession that involves nurturing and supporting others and engaging in creative lesson planning. Pisceans were particularly likely to choose teaching roles where they work with very young students, and such professions are best suited to those with compassionate, generous, helpful natures.

Pisceans may be less likely to become bakers because many are sensitive to certain ingredients or because they feel trapped when forced to spend their time in a single room all day. They may also dislike being painters because this work rarely provides opportunities to be creative, and the chemicals in industrial paints may cause negative reactions, as many Pisceans have chemical sensitivities. This vulnerability to negative reactions may also rule out chemistry, furniture making, and hairdressing for many Pisceans.

As for bank clerks, most Pisceans lack the extroversion required for this profession and they have a strong aversion to exacting, detail-oriented work that requires adding up numbers and filling in forms.

Crime

Sachs also gathered crime statistics for the twelve sun signs, finding that Pisceans were slightly more likely than those of other signs to be convicted of drug dealing, driving without a license, and hit and run, and less likely to be convicted of drug use.

Chapter 12: Pisces Stuff

The following things are associated with the sign of Pisces.

Animals: eagle, elephant, seahorse, all fish

Metal: zinc

Foods: lime, chestnut, strawberry, currant, fig

Trees: oak, chestnut, birch, ash, alder, fig, willow

Plants and herbs: sage, water lily, aniseed, nutmeg, marjoram, balm, daisy, dandelion, kelp, white poppy, jonquil

Parts of the body: feet, lymphatic and glandular systems

Number: 7

Places: Portugal, Tanzania, Tonga, Seville, Alexandria, Casablanca, Lisbon, Dublin

Gemstones: bloodstone, quartz stone, pearl, lapis lazuli, amethyst (February), aquamarine (March)

Colors: sea green, ocean blue, lilac, white, silver, violet

Patterns or design motifs: gentle curving patterns, ocean motifs, rolling wave or cloud patterns, smoke patterns, ripples, softly blending colors (rather than sharp delineations), natural/spiritual/mystical themes

Other Pisces associations:

- alcoholic beverages
- art
- boats
- costumes or disguises
- dance
- glasswork
- healing/hospitals
- masks
- mermaids
- movies
- music
- mysticism
- painting/paints
- photographs
- places of seclusion or confinement
- poetry
- seashells
- secrets and secret societies
- songs
- spirituality
- storytelling
- the subconscious mind
- water
- wigs

Appendix 1: Famous Pisceans

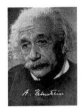

Famous people with the sun in Pisces include:

- Adam Levine
- Aidan Quinn
- Aileen Wuornos
- Alan Rickman
- Albert Einstein
- Alexander Graham Bell
- Anais Nin
- Ansel Adams
- Antonio Vivaldi
- Arthur Schopenhauer
- B.F. Skinner
- Billy Corgan
- Billy Crystal
- Bobby Fischer
- Bobby Orr
- Bruce Willis
- Carrie Underwood
- Carrot Top
- Charles Ponzi
- Chelsea Clinton
- Chelsea Handler
- Chuck Norris
- Cindy Crawford
- Dakota Fanning
- Dane Cook
- Daniel Craig
- David Gilmour
- David Niven

- Dennis Rader
- Douglas Adams
- Dr. Seuss
- Drew Barrymore
- Ed McMahon
- Edgar Cayce
- Edward Albee
- Elizabeth Barrett Browning
- Elizabeth Taylor
- Ellen Page
- Emily Blunt
- Enrico Caruso
- Eva Longoria
- Eva Mendes
- Fabio
- Fats Domino
- Floyd Mayweather Jr.
- Frank Gehry
- Fred (Mr.) Rogers
- Freddie Prinze Jr.
- Frederic Chopin
- Gabriel Garcia Marquez
- George Frideric Handel
- George Harrison
- George Washington
- Gilbert Gottfried
- Glenn Close
- Glenn Miller
- Gloria Vanderbilt
- Harriet Tubman
- Harry Belafonte
- Henrik Ibsen
- Henry Wadsworth Longfellow
- Jack Kerouac
- Jackie Gleason
- James Earl Ray
- Jean Harlow
- Jeff Kinney
- Jennifer Love Hewitt
- Jerry Lewis
- Jessica Biel
- Jimmy Swaggart
- John Herschel
- John Steinbeck

- John Updike
- John Wayne Gacy
- Johnny Cash
- Jon Bon Jovi
- Justin Bieber
- Kathy Ireland
- Kato Kaelin
- Kelsey Grammer
- Kesha Sebert
- Khaled Hosseini
- Kurt Cobain
- Kurt Russell
- L. Ron Hubbard
- Lawrence Welk
- Lee Marvin
- Levi Strauss
- Linus Pauling
- Liza Minnelli
- Lois Lowry
- Lord Baden-Powell
- Lou Costello
- Lou Reed
- Luther Burbank
- Matthew Flinders
- Maurice Ravel
- Michael Bisping
- Michael Caine
- Michelangelo Buonarroti
- Mikhail Gorbachev
- Mitt Romney
- Nat King Cole
- Nicolai Rimsky-Korsakov
- Nicolaus Copernicus
- Nina Simone
- Oliver Wendell Holmes
- Olivia Wilde
- Osama Bin Laden
- Patricia Hearst
- Pierre-Auguste Renoir
- Pope Pius XII
- Prince Albert II of Monaco
- Queen Latifah
- Quincy Jones
- Rachel Weisz
- Ralph Nader

- Ranulph Fiennes
- Rex Harrison
- Richard Ramirez
- Rick Perry
- Rihanna
- Rob Lowe
- Rob Reiner
- Robert Mugabe
- Roger Daltry
- Ron Howard
- Rudolph Nureyev
- Rue McClanahan
- Rupert Murdoch
- Sean Astin
- Sharon Stone
- Sidney Poitier
- Spike Lee
- Steve Irwin
- Steve Jobs
- Tammy Faye Bakker
- Ted Kennedy
- Tommy Tune
- Tony Iommi
- Tony Randall
- Tony Robbins
- Trevor Noah
- Vanessa Williams
- Victor Hugo
- W. H. Auden
- Wyatt Earp
- Yuri Gagarin

Pisces Rising (Pisces Ascendant)

The ascendant is the mask we wear in social situations, or the outer persona we show to others. In the case of Pisces rising, the external personality will be defined by Pisces traits, or a blend between Pisces and the sun sign.

Famous people with Pisces rising include:

- Alexander Graham Bell
- Antonio Banderas
- Carol Burnett
- David Carradine
- Diane Keaton
- George Clooney
- Gwyneth Paltrow
- Herbie Hancock
- Jason Alexander
- Julie Kavner
- Oliver Hardy
- Pierre Curie
- Richard Pryor
- Ringo Starr
- Robert Redford
- Tom Jones
- Vincent Price
- Whitney Huston

Appendix 2: Moon Signs, Ascendants (Rising Signs), and Other Planets

The natal zodiac is like a snapshot of the sky at the moment of birth. Astrologers believe that planetary placements and aspects at the time of birth influence personality and fortune. The sun, moon, and ascendant (rising sign) are the primary astrological forces, though planets also play a role.

Astrodienst (www.Astro.com) offers free chart calculation, so you can use this site to find your planetary placements and aspects and your rising sign (for the rising sign, you will need your time of birth as well as the date and place).

The Most Significant Astrological Forces

Most people know their Sun sign, which is the zodiac position of the sun at the time of birth, but few know their rising or moon signs or where their angular planets lie. In fact, the majority of people are surprised to learn that they even have these things.

Of the planetary placements, the sun, moon, and rising signs have the strongest effect on personality. The other planetary placements (positions of the planets at the time of birth) also have effects, though these are not as strong and tend to be concentrated in certain areas rather than shaping the entire personality.

The Sun Sign: The sun sign provides information about basic character and a framework for the rest of the natal zodiac. However, other elements such as the rising sign (also known as the ascendant) and moon sign affect the way the sun sign is expressed.

The Rising Sign (Ascendant): The rising sign determines the outward expression of personality, or the way in which a person interacts with the external world. It can be described as the public persona or mask. It also indicates how an individual is likely to be perceived by others (how he or she comes across socially).

When the sun and ascendant are in the same or similar signs, a person behaves in a way that is consistent with his or her inner character. When the rising sign is very different from the sun sign, the individual is likely to be pulled in competing directions or to send out signals that don't match inner feelings, which increases the likelihood of being misunderstood by others. While such conflicts can make life difficult, they are also a source of creativity and a spur to achievement.

The Moon Sign: The moon sign is the private persona, only seen in adulthood by those very close to the person. The moon rules over childhood and people are more likely to express their moon sign personalities when they are young. In adulthood, the moon's influence is usually hidden, relegated to the secret emotional life, though an individual may openly express the moon sign persona in times of stress or other emotional extremes.

The moon also represents the mother and other female forces in a person's life. The placement of the moon in a natal chart can indicate the types of relationships and interactions a person is likely to have with women.

Other Planets

Other planets also play a role in shaping the qualities that make up an individual. Each of the planets has a particular sphere of influence, and its effects will be determined by the sign in which the planet falls and the aspects it makes to other planets.

Mercury: all forms of mental activity and communication, including speaking and writing, the intellect, intelligence, reason, perception, memory, understanding, assimilation of information, and critical thinking

Venus: love, affection, pleasure, beauty, sex appeal, art, romantic affairs, adornment, social graces, harmony, and friendship

Mars: physical energy, will power, temper, assertiveness, boldness, competitiveness, impulsiveness, forcefulness, aggression, action, accidents, destructiveness, courage, and sex drive

Jupiter: luck and fortune, optimism, generosity, expansiveness, success, higher education, law, medicine, philosophy, abundance, and spirituality

Saturn: hard work, responsibility, character, strength of will, endurance, hard karma, difficulties, obstacles, hardship, the ability to see a task through to completion, authority, diligence, limitations, self-control, stability, patience, maturity, restriction, and realism

Uranus: progressiveness, change, originality, invention, innovation, technology, science, rebellion, revolution, sudden events and opportunities, awakenings, shocks, flashes of genius, eccentricity, unconventionality, unusual circumstances or events, independence, visionary ideas, and occult interests

Neptune: imagination, intuition, mysticism, dreams, fantasies, compassion, psychic abilities, visions, spirituality, strange events, the subconscious, repressed memories, glamour, mystery, insanity, drama, addiction, ideals, inspiration, transcendence, artistic sensibilities, and creative genius

Pluto: power, transformation, release of dormant forces, change, the subconscious, suppressed energies, death, rebirth, regeneration, sex, jealousy, passion, obsession, intensity, creation and destruction, beginnings and endings that occur simultaneously (one thing ending so that another can begin), secrets, mystery, undercurrents, precognition, personal magnetism, and extremes of personality

House Placements

House placements are a sort of fine tuning, adding some small, specific details about the ways in which various planetary placements will be expressed. The planets represent the spheres of life in which the sign traits are acted out, and the house placements are the stage or setting for these acts.

1st House: self-awareness and self-expression, outer personality, responses to outside stimuli, assertiveness, competitiveness, self-promotion, and courses of action chosen (ruled by mars)

2nd House: material possessions and attitude towards material possessions and money, ability to earn money, extensions of material wealth such as quality of food, decadence, luxury, and physical or external beauty (ruled by Venus)

3rd House: logical and practical reasoning, the intellect, agility, dexterity, curiosity, all forms of communication, all forms of media, intuition about trends and public desires or tendencies, short journeys, and siblings (ruled by Mercury)

4th House: home and hearth, domestic life, domestic chores, family, babies, comfort, the mothering instinct, food, and household items (ruled by the moon)

5th House: creative self-expression, socializing, children, early education, sports, the arts (especially the performing arts), pleasure and places of amusement, parties, social popularity, amd fame (ruled by the sun)

6th House: necessary tasks, details, health consciousness, nutrition, humility, hard work, organization, service, self-control, and sense of duty (ruled by Mercury)

7th House: relationships, friendships, marriage, all forms of partnership (business and social), harmony, balance, conflict avoidance, sense of justice, ideals, the reactions of others to our actions, what attracts us to other people (the sign at the beginning of our seventh house is often the astrological sign we find most attractive), fairness, and aesthetic sense (ruled by Venus)

8th House: legacies, shared resources, taxes, power, death, rebirth, sexuality, the dark side of life, deep psychology, personal magnetism, transformation (self-initiated or imposed by external forces), secrets or secret societies, spying, and prophetic dreaming (ruled by Pluto)

9th House: long distance travel, higher education, religion, medicine, law, animals, knowledge gained through travel and philosophical thinking, high ideals, philanthropy, luck, expansiveness, and ideas about social justice and civilization (ruled by Jupiter)

10th House: career, responsibility, honor and dishonor, perceptions of authority, relationships with authority figures, relationships with business and political power structures, responsibility, hard work, limitations, social standing, public reputation, and business (ruled by Saturn)

11th House: humanitarian endeavors, social ideals, group work, intellectual creative expression, desire to change social and political structures, contrariness, rebelliousness, invention and innovation, progressiveness, change, and personal freedom (ruled by Uranus)

12th House: the subconscious mind, self-sacrifice, intuition, miracles, secret knowledge, martyrdom, spiritual joy and sorrow, imagination, dreams, brilliance, madness, sensation-seeking, self-destruction, addiction, compassion, kindness, the ability to transcend boundaries, confusion, deception (of others and oneself), and altruism (ruled by Neptune)

Angular Planets

Angular planets are planets located along the axis – in other words, planets that fall along the line where the 12th house joins the 1st house, the 3rd house joins the 4th house, the 6th house joins the 7th house, and the 9th house joins the 10th house. Of these, the line that separates the 12th house from the 1st house and the line that separates the 9th house from the 10th house are considered the most important.

Planets that fall where the 12th house joins the 1st house will have a particularly strong effect on overall personality. Planets at this location are called rising planets, so a person with Uranus on the cusp of the 12th and 1st houses will be strong in the areas ruled over by Uranus and show traits of the sign that Uranus rules (Aquarius).

Planets located on the midheaven, which is the cusp of the 9th and 10th houses, also have a very strong effect on certain aspects of personality, particularly career aptitudes and choices. Rising and midheaven planets are some of the most important factors in a person's chart, though IC planets (those located on the cusp of the 3rd and 4th houses) and descending planets (located on the cusp of the 6th and 7th houses) can also have an effect.

The IC provides insights into the self that is seen by those closest to us, such as family, as well as our family structure.

The descendant, or cusp of the 6th and 7th houses, indicates the sorts of people we are attracted to. Theoretically, we should be most attracted to the sign of our descendant (directly opposite our ascendant).

Some astrologers believe that people who have many angular planets are more likely to become famous at some point during their lives.

Aspects

Aspects are the angles the planets formed in relation to one another at the time of a person's birth. The aspects considered most important include the conjunction, sextile, square, trine, inconjunct, and opposition.

Conjunction: A conjunction occurs when two planets are 0 degrees apart – in other words, right next to one another. This powerful aspect is often beneficial, though not always, because if the two planets involved are in negative aspect to many other planets, the conjunction can intensify the problems associated with the difficult aspects.

Planets in conjunction are working together, and their influence will have a major effect on personality. People with planets in conjunction often have one or two extremely well-developed talents or aptitudes, and many people who invent things or are responsible for medical breakthroughs have conjunctions or stelliums (more than two planets in conjunction). Having three or more planets in conjunction can indicate genius in a certain area.

Sextile: A sextile occurs when two planets are 60 degrees apart. Sextiles are beneficial aspects that create opportunities.

Unlike the trine, which simply drops good fortune in a person's lap, the sextile presents opportunities in the areas ruled by the planets involved in the sextile, and it is up to the individual to seize these opportunities and make something of them.

Square: A square occurs when two planets are 90 degrees apart. Squares are stressful or challenging aspects.

Having squares in a natal chart often encourages creativity and ambition, as squares bring obstacles that must be overcome and strife that inspires the individual to develop necessary strengths and use creative problem-solving abilities. Squares can promote character development because they ensure that life never becomes too easy.

Trine: Trines occur when two planets are 120 degrees apart. Trines are the most positive and harmonious aspects, bringing good fortune, ease, advantage, and luck in the areas ruled over by the planets involved in the trine.

Inconjunct (Quincunx): An inconjunct occurs when two planets are 150 degrees apart. The effects of the inconjunct are unpredictable, though often problematic.

An inconjunct can indicate stress, health problems, weaknesses, challenges, and obstacles in the personality or the environment that must be overcome. Some astrologers believe that the inconjunct (also known as a quincunx) brings the types of challenges that create wisdom.

Opposition: An opposition occurs when two planets are 180 degrees apart. Oppositions are difficult aspects that can bring discord, stress, chaos, and irritation, but like squares they tend to promote creativity, strength, and character development. It is more productive to view them as challenges rather than problems.

References

Bugler, C. (Ed.). (1992). *The Complete Handbook of Astrology*. Marshall Cavendish Ltd., Montreal.

Castille, D. (2000). *Sunny Day for a Wedding*. Les Cahiers du RAMS.

Fenton, S. (1989). *Rising Signs*. HarperCollins, London.

Heese, A. (2017). Cafe Astrology. CafeAstrology.com.

Quigley, J.M. (1975). *Astrology for Adults*. Warner Books, New York.

Rowe, P. *The Health Zodiac*. Ashgrove Press, Bath.

Sachs, G. (1998). *The Astrology File: Scientific Proof of the Link Between Star Signs and Human Behavior*. Orion Books, London.

Woolfolk, J.M. (2001). *The Only Astrology Book You'll Ever Need*. Madison Books, Lanham, MD.

Image Credits

Pisces fish: publicdomainvectors.org

All other images were obtained from publicdomainfiles.com:

- A pair of hearts: Mogwai
- Alianças (rings): Adassoft
- Broken heart: Maqndon
- Building: Master Sgt. Terry L. Blevins, US Air Force
- Business people silhouettes: Asrafil
- Painting: Dream of Italy by William Louis Sonntag, 1859, Dayton Art Institute
- Eagle: Dave Menke
- Einstein: US Department of Energy
- Faces: Inky2010
- Father walking with his children: CDC/Amanda Mills
- Gardening: Lance Cheung, USDA
- Hands with hearts: Petr Kratochvil
- Hearts: Vera Kratochvil
- Jigsaw: Yuri196
- Love of books: George Hodan
- Night sky with moon and stars: George Hodan
- Oak: US EPA
- Penguins: Merlin 2525
- Stethoscope: Johnny_automatic
- Strawberry: Anna Langova
- Water lily: Hana Muchova
- Young girl playing on the beach: CDC/Amanda Mills

Made in the USA
Las Vegas, NV
27 February 2022

44674516R00074